What successful entrepreneurs say about
The Worst Business Model in the World

We're in a special moment in history that finds every major category under pressure of reinvention. One of those definition reinventions is Entrepreneurship, and Danny's personal view articulated within the pages of *The Worst Business Model in the World* is a unique, engaging, and fun look at change. A definition of entrepreneurship that's more human, personal, and approachable.
— **Charles Adler, Co-founder, Kickstarter**

As an entrepreneur (or entrepreneur wanna-be), have you felt crazy creative, like you can't quite fit in with the formally structured way things are done? Like you love what you do but your family's always on your case to stop acting so strangely? You might just be a UDOT! If you are—or if you live with one you love—Danny Schuman's new book will be an eye-opener, maybe even a life saver! If this sounds like you, *The Worst Business Model in the World* will show you very clearly that, despite what may seem to be the opposite, UCAN succeed like never before!
— **Ari Weinzweig, Co-owner and Founding Partner, Zingerman's**

If you're a current or aspiring entrepreneur with a great idea in your head but no formal business training in your background, you should read this book. It's a fun and easy read with great tips in every chapter and worksheets that help you use them right away. Having no business background myself, I wish it was around when I started Threadless!
— **Jake Nickell, Founder, CEO, Threa**

Wanna be an entrepreneur but the idea scares this book. Danny breaks entrepreneurship dow.. ... actionable way that I couldn't help but giggle my way through the book while scribbling notes. It's so loaded with helpful information that I'm recommending it to every single one of our 11,500 mom entrepreneurs in The Founding Moms Community. Go on, read it. You'll thank me later. (And possibly Danny, too.)

> — Jill Salzman, Founder, The Founding Moms, Author of *Found It*, Co-host, Breaking Down Your Business podcast

Clearly Danny Schuman is not a born entrepreneur, and I mean that in a good way. He's a writer by trade and also an entrepreneur who started a successful business. So he learned a ton as he figured it out and the tips he provides are very creative, somewhat unorthodox, and highly actionable. It's a must-read with great insights for any current or future entrepreneurs.

> — Gregg Latterman, Founder/CEO Aware Records, Adjunct Professor, Northwestern University Innovation and Entrepreneurship

Danny Schuman has spent his time in the trenches as an entrepreneur. In *The Worst Business Model in the World*, he uses that experience to act as coach, teacher, pragmatic optimist and standup comedian, nudging and cajoling readers to believe in their value and showing them what they can do differently, right now, to experience more success. Reading this book made me smile, because it's not just about succeeding as an entrepreneur, it's about succeeding as a person.

> — Claire Lew, Founder/CEO, Know Your Company

Danny Schuman shows how well he knows entrepreneurs in this informative, enjoyable, and incredibly helpful book. His insights are spot on, illustrated with relatable stories, and brought to life with fresh and practical tools. Put simply, this book is a great resource for entrepreneurs craving to be both happy and profitable.

> — Jason Hull, Serial Entrepreneur and Investor, Founder/CEO, Balanced Edge, President, Practical Business Consulting

The Worst Business Model in the World

A New Kind of Guide for a New Kind of Entrepreneur

Danny Schuman

Published by Cortado Press

Cover and illustrations designed by Jess Hanebury
Formatting by Polgarus Studio

www.WBMITW.com
www.heyudots.com
www.twistyourthinking.com

ISBN-13 978-0692068526
ISBN-10 069206852X

To Wendy, for infinite patience, love, acceptance, and wisdom, and for making sure I don't leave the house dressed like an idiot.

Contents

Preamble
The Who, the Why, and the How

If you're an entrepreneur or an aspiring entrepreneur whose sole purpose in life is amassing money, this book is not for you. Please close it right now.

If you're an entrepreneur or an aspiring entrepreneur craving the flexibility to be passionate, original, and unabashedly enthusiastic about what you do, set aside the time and space to look at life through the prism of What Could Be, and do work that excites you on a daily basis, while—importantly—still making enough money to not have to worry about money, *The Worst Business Model in the World* may be calling your name.

If you wake up every day hoping to create something that could benefit you, the people you love, or even people you don't know and may never meet, while maintaining the ability to think strategically about your business so you can stay in business—I'm so glad this book found you. Please read on.

Some entrepreneurs toil and sweat and stress so they can create the next Facebook, Instagram, or Snapchat and cash out. I don't begrudge them but I also don't share that philosophy. I don't want to be the next Mark Zuckerberg. I just want to be the first me.

I want to be happy doing what I'm good at on a daily basis and still be financially secure. I'd like to live soulfully and also profitably. Fill my wallet and feed my heart. For the past 10 years, I've been able to do this because—or despite—I have what I think might be the worst business model in the world.

So, I'm an entrepreneur, I suppose.

But more than that, I'm a UDOT. And if you're still reading, you're probably a UDOT too.

UDOT: **U**s **D**oing **O**ur **T**hing. Pronounced "Yu-daht."

UDOTs work for ourselves instead of working for the (Wo)Man. We do what we're good at and are passionate about. However, we're pretty unenthusiastic about—and sometimes incompetent at—the more technical aspects of doing what we love, things like business development, finance, administration, and legal responsibilities.

We're programmers, musicians, lawyers, accountants, authors, designers, custom tailors, taco stand owners, dog walkers, psychiatrists, and multitudes of other professionals on our own who could use a little help with what doesn't come naturally: the part of having a business where we have to run a business.

Sometimes we make grand plans and don't fulfill them. Other times we set a clear vision but make no plans, feeling our way and hoping we get there. Once in a while we have no plan and no vision, but we have passion and determination, so we put one brain cell in front of the other and trust that something good will come of it.

It may be a terrible business model, but it's a wonderful existence.

Being an entrepreneur is more planned and financially based; being a UDOT is more about being in the moment. If the plan doesn't unfold exactly as you hoped, that's part of the beauty. We're here to make our souls happy and our bank accounts full enough to continue doing what we love. For an entrepreneur, straying too far from the curvature of Profit and Loss is a problem. For a UDOT, taking the path that's right in front of you is a glorious opportunity.

UDOTs embrace that freedom. We get bored easily. We crave new challenges that introduce us to different people and projects, because they create the potential for new and unexpected ideas. On the other hand, it often means more project-based work, which means more hustling and less security. It may not be such a good business model, but it enables us to come up with new ideas and solve new problems. That's exciting to us.

We get to experience what one UDOT called "the prosperity in there." The good stuff inherent to being on our own. The flexibility to set our own schedules and spend more time with our kids. The ability to pursue our passions. Having Yes or No be our choice, based on what's best for the people and the project, not politics. Instead of making our way from meeting to meeting, we have the time to think freely and create the next great thing.

We get to spend more time doing the things we love and less time doing the things we hate.

In our UDOT world, where challenges are seldom the same from day to day, how can we build a model or a process to help us succeed? Whatever it is has to have the flexibility to adapt in an always-changing world. We each need to have the ability to create our own best version of a Worst Business Model.

The method to the madness

To help you create your own best Worst Business Model, I've broken this book into five categories, each with a number of tips to help you succeed as a UDOT. The categories are therefore called **W**ays UDOTs **W**in, or WUWs. Pronounced, of course "Woooos!"

You can use them in three different ways.

The first is to use them randomly. A lot of us don't need or even want a plan. You know who you are, you "Ready Fire Aim!" school of thought-ers. If you're guided by any rule, it's the rule of "We'll figure it out." If that's you, using this book is easy: just open the book to any page, see if it applies to where you are today, and try putting that tool into action. If it's not applicable or doesn't work today, try turning to a different WUW and page. Do the same thing tomorrow and try a different tool. A lot of the UDOTs I talked to think this is a pretty valid system. So much of our lives as UDOTs is instinctive. Trial and error. See what works, keep doing it if it does, try something different if it doesn't.

The second way to use the WUWs is to choose depending on what's up in your world.

- If you're experiencing the kind of day or work situation where you need a good personal kick in the pants, *you'll want to focus on the first WUW.*
- If you need to believe the world is behind you and pay attention to that possibility, *try the second WUW.*
- If you're feeling alone out here, in need of companionship or partnership, someone to share your pain, *that's the third WUW.*
- If you're stuck and don't know what to do to keep things moving forward, *go to the fourth WUW.*
- If you need a reminder of why we're doing what we're doing and how supremely awesome it is that we're able to do this, even if the day that just passed really sucked, *the fifth WUW* is for you. The fifth WUW is a reminder to enjoy the fruits of our labor.

The third way is the anti-randomizer: using the WUWs to create a concrete plan as a logical way forward. This may be especially applicable if you're just getting going, or if you've been around for a while but are in a crucial place where you really need to examine what you're doing and what might come next—also known as a pivot. When you're in one of those situations, the WUWs provide an order. Start with the first and progress sequentially through the rest of the WUWs. Let them lead you. It's a great way to create a path to success with steps you can chart out and see. A map to show you the way from Point A to Point Be Awesome.

This probably won't surprise you, but I firmly believe you don't have to stick closely to any one of these three ways to use the WUWs. "A UDOT may not necessarily have a plan," said Stacy Elsbury, a UDOT and the owner of a pioneering consumer research company. "For me, I'm appreciative that I have this day, and may be able to anticipate tomorrow. But as far as next week goes, I don't know. So today, I'm in."

Me too. Get in line, put in your order and see where it takes you.

The soul-warming promise
of life as a UDOT

There are hundreds of thousands of UDOTs in the world, and that number is steadily growing.[1] I've had the incredible pleasure of interviewing dozens of them as I wrote this book. They described their journeys with equal parts passion and pragmatism, acknowledging the pitfalls and celebrating the possibilities. They regret nothing and don't look back.

When talking about the freedom he feels as a UDOT, Scott Hughes, a consumer insights expert, said, "It means occasional moments of panic when you realize there's no IT department, but frequent moments of relief when you realize there's no HR department."

"Security is a false promise," said David JP Fisher, a sales coach who facetiously called himself "completely unemployable." He's much more comfortable and confident on his own instead of relying on an employer to make his life secure.

Keith Glantz runs a web design firm and affirmed his decision to be a UDOT like this: "If I was out there chasing the dollar I would've become an investment banker. I'm willing to sacrifice profit margin for happiness."

And speaking for most UDOTs, Claire Lew, who created software that helps businesses better understand their employees, described what's at the heart of

---

[1] 2015 Kauffman Index (https://www.fastcompany.com/3046773/hit-the-ground-running/the-state-of-the-american-entrepreneur-in-2015)

it: "It enables us to do the most with what we have. It's the purest form of problem-solving."

Interviewing UDOTs provided many of the insights for this book. It was exciting because of everything I learned, and it was awesome because it confirmed the fact that as a UDOT, I've found my tribe.

Like many of you, I started a small company despite having no formal business training and barely any business acumen. But I was full of unending passion and (probably unwarranted) optimism. To top it off, I started my marketing consultancy Twist in January 2009, in the heart of the most awful economic doldrums of the past 75 years. To paraphrase Gloria Gaynor, I survived. Thrived, even.

I didn't create an app that was acquired for 100 million dollars and I don't have a company that was named one of *Inc*'s top 50 startups. I only have one degree, a super un-functional BA in political science (with honors!). I don't even have a minor.

I haven't done much planning or modeling. Most of the planning I do revolves around lunch and coffee. The only modeling I could do would be in a clothing catalogue for men with a little potbelly who still want to look somewhat cool.

I built and grew my network without a Salesforce-type app or CRM system. I rely on diligence, humor and a pretty good memory.

I mostly run my business by the seat of my pants and the usually reliable synapses of my brain. My plan would best be described as a do-good-work, figure-it-out-as-I-go kind of plan.

If that's not the worst business model in the world, I don't know what is.

Thing is, it's worked. Despite having all the pre-requisites for a failed business, Twist endures.

We work with small local clients and Fortune 500 global clients, B2B, B2C, B2whoever. Great projects have stretched my brain, expanded my skill sets, and established relationships with people who are now not just trusted clients but genuine friends.

In that time I've also put one and five-eighths kids through college at the University of Michigan, where tuition's about the same as buying a private Caribbean island. I eat and drink well, I travel far enough away and sleep on nice-enough thread count sheets. I get to wear somewhat cool clothes. Our dog and cat seem pretty happy.

And maybe most important, I've spent more time doing the things I love than the things I hate.

I've kept great notes as I progressed through the ups and downs of starting and growing Twist, and I learned new lessons almost every day. Sometimes joyfully, sometimes painfully. I paid attention to what worked and what flopped, and as the years passed and my business prospered, I recorded those business-building lessons. They became more codified as I talked to dozens of other UDOTs.

Those lessons formed the backbone of this primer on how to succeed in business without instinctively being any good at it. *The Worst Business Model in the World* is designed to help all of the so-close-to-being-successful, pretty-consistently-successful, and ridiculously-successful-but-maybe-also-kind-of-sometimes-lying UDOTs in the world.

To all current and future UDOTs, this book's for you.

Stacy Elsbury, one of my favorite UDOT interviewees, ended our session by saying, "I was never meant to be a business person. I was always meant to be a UDOT." She just latched onto something she loved doing, and figured out a way to do it really well.

Being out on our own and living in a world of uncertainty can genuinely feel like a terrible business model with a low chance of success. This book will reassure you that you're not alone and provide the tools to use when that feeling hits and you need help.

When I first started writing this book, I thought it would just be for creative professionals like writers and designers. But when I told a friend about it, she said, "Omigod, that's my husband!" Her husband's a lawyer. And a UDOT.

I found the same to be true for people in logistics, online printing, recruiting, wellness coaching, sports memorabilia, nursing, healthcare analytics, and not-for-profits. As you can imagine, the list goes on and on.

If you're out on your own doing your thing, trying to figure out how to make it work on a daily basis, this book is for you.

If you're not a UDOT yet, this book is for you too. You may be dying to go out on your own but you're nervous that you won't be able to pull it off. Well, get used to it. That nervousness will stay with you for the rest of your UDOT life. But so will the energy, the excitement, the fulfillment, the passion, the joy, and the rush of blood to your heart when you accomplish something great.

Whether you're a veteran UDOT or on your way to becoming one, I hope this book helps you be as not sucky at business as possible, so you can do all the things you're so good at with less pain and more joy. I hope it helps you eat well, travel well, and maybe even buy your own (small but with great weather) private island.

Onward and forward.

THE FIRST WUW
TRUST YOURSELF

Where you have faith in the value you bring

You'll get there.

There may be times in your journey as a UDOT when it feels like you're being betrayed by gravity, floating aimlessly, directionless, untethered, seemingly not getting any closer to the place you call success. Where once you were ok with a bumpy ride, now you're not sure if you're ever going to get where you're going. You may even have to return to a previous existence, aka a "real job."

Even in the face of debilitating doubt, it's important for UDOTS to have ass-kicking confidence in what we bring to every opportunity. Have faith that how we do what we do is the right way to do it. When it works—and it will work—you'll have evidence that you can use in the future to remind yourself that you've succeeded in the past.

The first **W**ay UDOTs **W**in is by constantly reminding yourself of your specialness and the value that you bring to the world. Don't think you're lucky to get work. Think that whoever hires you is lucky to have you.

Knowing that there are many versions of yourself, try to be the best one as often as possible. Trust yourself. You've got this.

Chapter 1
Ask for the money

Ah, the money part. That's a good place to begin. Estimating it, charging it, collecting it, and most important, getting paid what we're worth. It's one of the biggest potential confidence-shaking, nausea-inducing elements of being a UDOT. But it's also a huge opportunity to start understanding and embracing the value of what we bring.

The bottom line? We'll make the money we let people pay us. You'll never charge enough unless you push yourself out of your "I'm not worthy" zone. The best advice I ever got? Do the best job you can to estimate the project, then come as close to doubling that number as you can tolerate.

Don't be afraid to do this. Don't feel bad if the potential client is someone you know. Don't think that client won't like you or give you any more work. If they approached you about a project, they won't walk away based on one proposal. If your fee scares them they'll tell you and you'll work it out. They won't think less of you for charging more. They'll appreciate the perceived value you'll bring.

And when you agree on a fee that seems exorbitant, even to you, the work you'll deliver will make everyone forget how much it cost. It'll validate your fee, and all will be good. All anyone will think is, "Great work! When can we do this again?!"

In my early years growing Twist, nobody told me I charged too much. Because I didn't charge enough! Consider the worst thing that can happen when you don't: you do an exceptional job (which of course you'll do) and look back at the work you did and the value you provided and the money you got paid, and depending on your preference in expletives, you'll say something to the effect of "?*&@#$%!!!"

It's true of sushi, toilet paper, and haircuts: clients get the quality they pay for and then suffer or enjoy the consequences. Since you're great at what you do and you'll do a great job at what they need, ask for the damn money. Prove your worth with excellent work, then go get more.

Worksheet:
Ask for the money

 ONE THING TO REMEMBER

You may be undercharging by up to half, so on your next proposal, ask for the maximum amount of money that won't make your stomach hurt.

 ONE THING TO DO

UDOT FEE CALCULATOR

_____ Start with the amount you figure is "fair" to charge potential client (AKA the amount that prompts her to pump her fist when she sees it)

_____ Multiply it by 2 (AKA "double")

_____ Subtract the amount that eases the nausea building in the pit of your stomach (if the nausea goes away completely you subtracted too much)

_____ Optimal fee for both you and client (what's really "fair")

TURN
WRONGS
INTO
RIGHTS

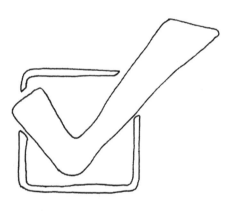

Chapter 2
Turn wrongs into rights

When something goes sideways, don't blame it on someone else. Acknowledge there's a problem and become part of the solution.

This is applicable even if the problem lies elsewhere. You can accrue a mountain of good feelings—and become a valuable partner—when you step up as the bigger person and help figure out a solution instead of shrinking into an unhappy whiny malcontent. Start asking questions right away. If finding where the blame lays helps to solve the problem, so be it, but make your first priority understanding the problem so you can be part of unearthing the brilliant solution.

A few years ago I facilitated a two-day marketing workshop for a longtime trusted client that was going well until her boss unexpectedly showed up partway through the first day. After observing for about an hour he took her aside and told her the workshop was ineffective and instructed her to pull the plug immediately. We gave the participants a break so the three of us could talk things over, and with a smile on my face I asked him what wasn't working. While patiently hearing him out I was able to hone in on an area that he agreed had promise to explore. After surviving the rest of day one I revised the day two agenda to focus on that area, and it helped accomplish both his goals and those of my client. Boxes double-checked, crisis averted, wrong turned into a right.

Even if a problem has devolved to DEFCON 1, be the optimist in the room. Challenge yourself to focus on nothing but positives and try to make things better. Remind yourself that you've learned a ton and have amazing talents to share and use with your clients.

Of course, things will go wrong. Digital marketing consultant Katherine Raz articulated the challenges of putting ourselves out there and the importance of reminding ourselves of the value we bring: "The best thing you can do when you're running a business is not take it too personally. Separate your personal worth from the success of the idea that you're trying to put into the world. It's not a reflection of your value whether the idea is successful or not. When you're on your own, you think, 'This is my life,' and your personal identity can get real wrapped up in it. You can lose all objectivity. So you have to stay diligent to not let that happen."

Remember that what we do has value. Help people to the best of your ability, and lead the charge to turn rotten tomatoes into delicious marinara. When something goes wrong, smile, take a deep breath, admit it and move on. You may or may not walk out an inch or two taller, but it might look that way to others.

Worksheet:
Turn wrongs into rights

Whether you're at the center of the problem or have nothing to do with it, when something goes wrong, smile and start asking questions so you can help make it right.

Practice turning wrongs into rights at home with friends or family by actively looking for situations where you can stay positive and fix things instead of making them worse. *This* is the paper you're handing in tomorrow? Why doesn't anybody clean up after themselves around here? Who ate the last damn cookie/slice of pizza/deviled egg? Do whatever it takes to pacify any pissed-off parties. Offer solutions to the problems, even if you had no part of causing them. Get good at making people love you even when they're not in the mood to like you.

Then write your answers to these questions:

What did you do?

How did it go?

How can you apply it to a "real" work situation?"

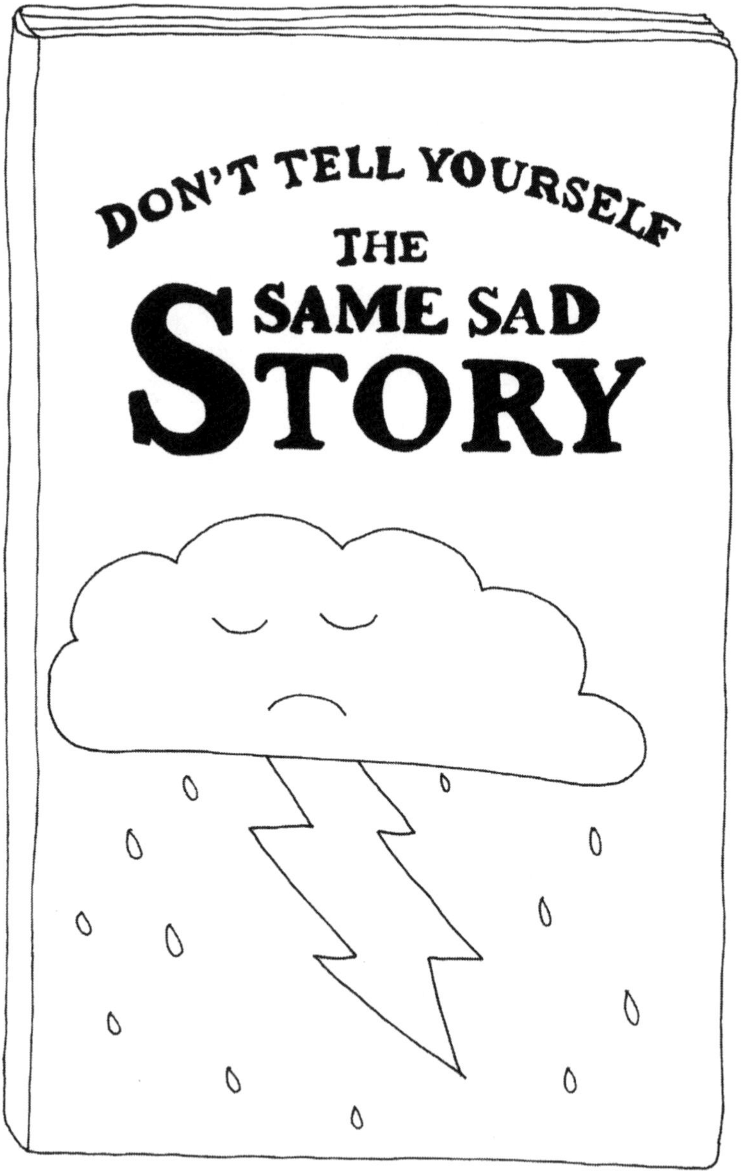
DON'T TELL YOURSELF
THE
SAME SAD
STORY

Chapter 3
Don't tell yourself the same sad story

If you do, it will become true.

I know UDOTs who fall into the trap of feeling sorry for themselves, who put the blame on other people, who are convinced the world is conspiring against them. Who hasn't felt that way at some point? We submit proposal after proposal and lose every one. Our best client gets fired, our best thinking partner takes a full-time job, our brilliant work gets lost in the shuffle of a corporate re-organization. When you're on your own and the bad stuff piles up, it's easy to start thinking there's a conspiracy against you. It's never true, but some UDOTs will start believing it. It's not just sad, it's detrimental to getting happy results. And UDOTs, we're way better than that.

When things get rocky, sidestep sob stories and create a new narrative, a really good, positive story with a cool beginning, awesome middle and awesomer ending. For the times when self-doubt creeps in, always have a story in your head from a time you were really successful and everything went right. End it with something like, "On this next project, I will absolutely blow away my client, and they will hug me and pay me and hire me again." That's a great story. Don't you love that story?

Here's another: Aaron Wolf is an ex-Marine and passionate outdoorsman who started an outdoors adventure company in Chicago. In a place where most of the action happens at local restaurants and bars, he's had big challenges convincing city people to drive four hours out of town to experience real wilderness. It doesn't deter him. "Even if it's a tough sell in

Chicago and the bottom line isn't good, I keep fighting, I never give up, and I count the wins," he said. "I'm not measured by my bankroll. If I feel like I've made an impact on others, then that's success." That's a great story too.

Get your great story together and tell it to yourself every day, every few minutes if you have to, so you start living and breathing it, and soon everyone else will too.

I could have spent years telling myself that I was at a disadvantage against the more traditional strategic consultants with whom I competed for projects, having no business background or formal business training. Instead, I developed a story as a strategic consultant with a creative background, with the advantage of being able to look at a problem from all sides and design more creative solutions. I love that story and a lot of my clients like it too. And here I am, in business 10 years later, still kicking butt.

Positivity is contagious and leads to more positive things. It also helps the world stay on your side. Don't be tempted by the not-so-happy side and get caught in a trap of negativity that you can't escape. A positive story on its own may not win business, but it will win people.

Worksheet:
Don't tell yourself the same sad story

 ONE THING TO REMEMBER

Always have a positive story about yourself ready to replay in your head to prevent bad stories from taking over.

 ONE THING TO DO

Repeat after me: "It's not my fault. I can't help it. It's not fair." Good, that's out of your system.

Now think about the last time you were brilliantly successful and write down three reasons you achieved that unqualified success.

1

2

3

Hey look! You have some good stuff to tell yourself the next time things get a little rocky.

Chapter 4:
Comparisons will kill you

No, your friend over there isn't necessarily doing way better than you because she's getting a venti caramel soy latte instead of a regular old coffee. Nor is your friend who just came back from two glorious weeks in Italy sipping wine and buying shoes. The coffee drinker may just really really like coffee; the world traveler could have dozens of ways she got to the Tuscan countryside. It's easy to make yourself crazy imagining everyone's doing better than you. They're not.

I'm outstanding at making up stories about people that seem plausible but most likely are far from the truth. One of my early mentors had tens of thousands of Twitter followers, a TED Talk under her belt, and was a featured speaker at tech events across the country. When I got to know her better I asked her how she got to be so successful. Her answer? "Once I start making money, I'll let you know."

You have no idea what anyone else is doing or how much they're making so don't assume they're killing it. You can certainly conjure up a doozy of a story that turns someone into the most envy-worthy person in the world. So take a deep breath and think about how things really are. "If I'm working and hopefully making the world a little better that's how I measure my success," said Sales Coach David JP Fisher. "Plus, I live next to a cemetery, so that provides good perspective."

It's so hard to maintain perspective and so easy to start comparing yourself to other people. It may happen most when we're light on work and have time on our hands to make up all kinds of crazy situations, and it is not healthy, not healthy indeed.

One sometimes difficult but positivity-rich option is to congratulate the world travelers, and ask the coffee drinkers if you can buy them a refill. Spend time with successful UDOTs. Get some of their magic to rub off on you. Ask questions, absorb their advice, use their knowledge. Don't get jealous, get smarter.

At a minimum, instead of comparing yourself to others in ways that are completely conjectured and unhealthy, compare yourself to yourself. Think about how great it felt when you were on fire and what you could be doing differently to get back to that place. Use those ideas and feelings as motivation to kick your own ass a little and get back to doing the amazing things that you're highly capable of doing.

Worksheet:
Comparisons will kill you

 ONE THING TO REMEMBER

Don't compare yourself to other UDOTs (or to anyone else). Ever. It never leads anywhere good.

 ONE THING TO DO

Get yourself a Positivity Buddy. You may have heard of Accountability Buddies, people who remind you of your promises and make sure you follow through. A Positivity Buddy reminds you how incredibly awesome you are and tells you something great about you every time you see them. (PS, you can have more than one.) Who's your first one?

My first Positivity Buddy: _____

Good! Now go pick up the phone and call her/him!

Chapter 5:
Be the first you

"Good artists borrow, great artists steal" has been attributed to many people, including Pablo Picasso and Igor Stravinsky. Regardless of where it came from, borrowing from experts who came before you is a great problem-solver for anyone trying to create something from scratch. Whether it's a new method, process, system, design, composition, font, code, or technique, paying attention to—and using—what's come before can be a massive help.

Japanese art of the mid-1800's influenced the impressionist painters. The Beatles were heavily influenced by Chuck Berry and Carl Perkins. Those artists borrowed from their predecessors to create their own ideas. There's power in using someone else's experience as a foundation to build on, to change and adapt, to reshape and reconstruct in a way that makes it your own. The danger is in trying to be or do something we admire; it's easy to fall into the trap of feeling pressured to be as good or insightful or "original" as those people.

I interviewed younger and older UDOTs for this book, and among the former, Claire Lew stood out. A few years out of college, she created Know Your Company, a software tool that helps business owners get to know their employees better and therefore run better companies. Her thoughts on gauging success were wise beyond her years: "I ask myself two things: Was I a good person? Did I try my best? If I can answer yes, then I sleep well." For us UDOTs, it doesn't have to be much more complicated than that.

My friend Amy Krouse Rosenthal was an incredibly special person who passed away far too soon. She created some amazing things in her life (go to whoisamy.com to see them). Above all, she was a hardworking and successful author. When I started writing *The Worst Business Model in the World*, I told her that my book would be kind of a Godin/Gladwell combo. She said, "Why not make it a Schuman original?"

Please please please don't stare at a famous classic work and crave the ability to do something exactly like it. You'll mostly drive yourself crazy with jealousy but you'll also rob yourself of bringing your awesomely cool voice to the world. Not to mention losing all that time trying to fit into someone else's skin when you've yet to break out of your own.

That book, that song, that code or system, those documents, those words and ideas— they're yours. They came from inside of you and that gives them credibility, meaning, and depth. Don't worry about becoming the next whoever. Focus on becoming the first you.

Worksheet:
Be the first you

 ONE THING TO REMEMBER

Use work created by people you admire as a guide, then create your own brilliance.

 ONE THING TO DO

Write down three people or groups of people who have created something you admire

1

2

3

The thing they created

1

2

3

What might it inspire you do to?

1

2

3

THE SECOND WUW
TRUST THE WORLD

Where you have faith that the world wants you to succeed

The world wants you to succeed. You can choose to believe it or not. But if you do, it's much more likely to come true. This is the second **W**ay **UDOTs Win**.

Regardless of how we imagine them or what we call them, UDOTS have to believe that there are forces at play beyond our control, waiting to help tip things in our favor. Again, if you don't believe this, it's less likely to happen.

UDOTs are aware, often painfully, that our journeys don't come with paychecks on the 15th and 31st of every month. We know that somewhere out there, there's something called Retirement, but we can't know how far away it is, or how much it costs to get there.

You're doing something that you love, or you're good at, or you care about, and you're the only one who can do what you do in the way that you do it. There's unlimited value in that. What you're doing has importance to the world and the world will pay you back.

You can worry all you want—and you'll probably worry a lot. I know I have. But I choose to believe what Mark Twain wrote: "Worrying is like paying a debt you don't owe."

You don't know what's going to happen. The world doesn't know either. Believe the world's on your side and it's a lot more likely to be something good.

Chapter 6:
Confidence = Generosity

Nothing is ever given away that isn't somehow eventually paid back. Be insanely big-hearted whenever possible; there are too many people out on their own not to help each other at every twist and turn.

If you have knowledge that could help someone else, give it away. Offer to send someone a sample proposal you've written. Help with billing and how much to charge. Provide websites with helpful tools. If you've learned anything on legal or financial matters, share that information with other UDOTs, especially when they're just starting out; it's invaluable to us because it's not our first language.

It's incredibly important to give your time, ideas, and resources, knowing it won't diminish you and can only help build up others.

After I lost my agency job and before I started Twist, I was the busiest creative entrepreneur (i.e., recently unemployed person) in the greater Chicago area. I burned a hole in my credit card taking people out for coffee and lunch, often four or five days a week. Instead of focusing solely on my field of marketing, I made it a point to meet with a wide variety of people, including salespeople, lawyers, facilitators, consultants, karate teachers, photographers, programmers, and data scientists.

Every meeting provided at least one useful nugget. One conversation, with an independent filmmaker, was especially helpful. I asked him about specializing vs. generalizing—finding a specific niche so people can easily understand what you do, vs offering a broad range of skill sets, which makes it harder to know how to think of you but also opens you up to more possibilities. He strongly advocated the latter and I agreed. Becoming a generalist didn't just help me increase my knowledge on a wide range of topics, it enabled me to procure enough work to sustain me for the first couple of years of Twist's existence.

Those people were extremely kind and generous with their time and knowledge. I know a lot of them were helping me because someone else had done the same for them. Now when someone invites me for a cup of coffee, regardless of the reason, I try as hard as I can to meet that person, even when I'm on a client deadline. I don't feel like I may be making a mistake, I feel like I may be doing something important. Serial entrepreneur Jason Hull, who has experienced tremendous success in his life, tells it this way: "A lot of people see the economy like pie, and if I get a bigger slice someone will get one smaller. I don't see it that way, as a limited number of pies. I see myself as a baker. The more I can bake the more people will get."

Confidence isn't selfish or insecure. It's generous. And often, it's contagious. Every time you agree to talk to someone over a salad or latte, you fuel internal positivity, and that's something you can't put a price on. It leads to brains being turned on, which leads to ideas being created, which leads to business improving. It's the most productive (and delicious) virtuous circle in the history of the world.

Worksheet:
Confidence = Generosity

 ONE THING TO REMEMBER

When you know something that could benefit another UDOT, give it away. It may not benefit you immediately, but it will eventually.

 ONE THING TO DO

List three veteran UDOTs who've given you valuable pieces of advice or information
1
2
3

List three newer UDOTs who could really use that information and share it with them
1
2
3

Chapter 7:
Don't chase ghosts

When I started Twist, I had a "Top Prospect" list of potential clients I was SURE I could count on for work. Mountains and mountains of work, so much work I'd have to open offices in New York, Los Angeles, and Dubai.

I never heard back from 80% of them.

But I kept sending them notes, calling them, spending precious time and energy trying to convince them to get back to me.

As a UDOT, it can be hard to walk away from a potential client when you think there may be even the slimmest of chances. Without a bi-monthly paycheck, we need to constantly sell our product or service to pay bills and keep the lights on. It's a sometimes tough and always true fact and it can lead us to want to make a sale so badly that we keep pursuing projects that don't really exist, going back to contacts that we know won't pan out. We send one more email, make one more call, hire one more skywriting airplane to write a message in the clouds imploring your "sure thing" to hire you already.

When that's the case, don't follow your heart, trust your brain. Pay attention to red flags that you may be seeing and ignoring. Do kickoff dates keep getting pushed back? Is the budget shrinking? Is there a mystery boss who needs to give the green light to the project but won't take a look at the proposal? You know where these are headed—nowhere—but you may not want to admit it.

Luckily, there's an awesome silver lining: For every ghost you chase, there's another potential client out there looking for someone with your talents. For every Top Prospect of mine who became a ghost and disappeared, I surprisingly found a wonderful client who I'd contacted with little hope of fulfillment, but who then became a longtime trusted partner. I can't explain it but I heard of similar experiences from many UDOTs.

"It's amazing how many people I never knew very well before who've become great clients," said Cindy Alston, a marketing strategist. "Sometimes they get back to me as soon as I send them a note and it often leads to a great project! It's weird but sometimes it just works that way."

When you can feel a prospect becoming a ghost, don't waste your valuable time chasing them down. Don't send one more email or leave one more voicemail (after weeks or months or even years of no responses), don't spend hours putting together a proposal that doesn't have a project attached to it. Don't do it. Your greatness will be lost on them. Your time is best spent on real opportunities where you can really bring your genius to life.

Worksheet:
Don't chase ghosts

 ONE THING TO REMEMBER

Focus your efforts on the opportunities that are most likely to pan out.

ONE THING TO DO

Start with the perfect project, expressed as a percentage	100%
If the potential client doesn't reply to three separate emails…	Subtract 10%
If the potential client continues to hold back project details…	Subtract 10%
If the potential client keeps pushing the start date later…	Subtract 10%
If something in your gut is telling you that it just doesn't feel right…	Subtract 25%
Total:	

If your total is under 75%, move on to your next great potential opportunity, whatever it may be.

Chapter 8:
If it doesn't fit, quit

I was suffering through a painfully slow period a few years into Twist's existence when I was approached to do a project that I immediately knew wasn't right for me. It wasn't ridiculously wrong. It was related to what I do. It just wasn't in my wheelhouse.

If I had been really busy I would've turned it down without hesitation. But I needed the work. So I convinced myself I could become an expert as I took the job and the work. I tirelessly researched the challenge, picked the brains of experts in the field, and studied the jargon of the business. But I never felt fully comfortable in my role, and as the project proceeded, I knew the people who hired me had their doubts as well.

Midway through the project I facilitated a meeting with 60 people who peppered me with questions that I didn't know how to answer. I may have studied the language but I wasn't anywhere near fluent in it, which was necessary to do the job well. The meeting went off the rails. We didn't come close to achieving the day's goals. The participants left the conference room frustrated and angry. I was fired the next day.

It was embarrassing to me and to the client and soured any chance I had to work with them on an appropriate project. It was completely avoidable.

There's almost nothing as gut-wrenchingly hard as turning down business. But if it doesn't feel right, say "no." It may be agonizing at the time, but pretty quickly, it'll feel right, and eventually, it'll feel great. And empowering. And business-building.

You instinctively know what's in your wheelhouse. It just feels different when you're working on something that feels right. "Any time I've been successful I've also been very happy, and it's when I'm working on things in my wheelhouse," said Kate Kimmerle, founder of a cosmetics company. "When I get out of that zone and veer off, it always bites me in the butt."

A lot of UDOTs are content to risk that butt-biting and take on every project, even when we know there's a high potential for time-stealing, soul-sucking, money-losing unhappiness. We'll say, "When I need the work, fake it 'til I make it." My experience has been "Fake it 'til the client and I get to a really unhappy place and I get fired and look like an idiot," which really isn't much fun at all. So now I say "Don't take it unless I'm pretty sure I can make it." There's a lot more happiness to be had when you start with that philosophy.

The world has other projects for you that fit your skill set much better. Focus your energies there rather than hoping you'll figure out something you have no idea how to do.

Worksheet:
If it doesn't fit, quit

ONE THING TO REMEMBER

ONE THING TO DO

(the book's only combo platter!):

Robert Evans, famous Hollywood movie producer and raconteur: "Every success I've had has been for a different reason, and every failure for the same...I've said yes when I should've said no."

When it comes to that moment when you know you should say "No" but are about to say "Yes," be Robert Evans.

Say "No."

THERE'S ALWAYS SOMETHING AROUND THE CORNER

Chapter 9:
There's always something around the corner

Sometimes the money runs out. It does, it happens.

Then the money comes back.

When the money's about to run out and the weight on your shoulders gets bigger than a two-ton elephant, remind yourself that the work has come before, and it will come again. Because it will. Even when it seems like it won't.

Whether you send out powerful brain waves, post on social media, or go all analogue on it and call friends and colleagues, tell the world you're out here and you're ready for another project. And while you're at it, let the world know what kind of project you want. What the hell, why not? If you're asking for something, you might as well get what you really want! Can't hurt.

When you get slow, or the work dries up, I've found that the most important thing to do is unquestionably the hardest thing to do: Combine your hard work with belief. Have faith. Defy the facts in front of your face and convince yourself that the next great project is within your reach. It's hard because it's so counterintuitive. The hardest time to be positive is when you have nothing to be positive about.

Digital marketing consultant Katherine Raz made a great analogy to being out at sea. "When you start anything, it's like you're swimming away from shore, and sometimes it keeps getting further and further away. Success is how long can you stay out there when you can't see land anymore."

When the bottom dropped out of my business for six months, it hurt to go to my co-working space and watch other people do business. Every day was hard and long and as the days passed they just got longer. So I turned to what I enjoy and do well: I wrote, mostly blog posts and posts on LinkedIn. Someone who read one of them contacted me because he was touched by the post. He didn't have a real need for my work but he created a little project. It was the snowflake that slowly snowballed into a succession of nice projects.

Whether it's a new job, an inspiring new collaborator, or a cool new spot for coffee, there's always something good around the corner. You can't see it yet, because, well, it's around the corner. It may take time, sometimes longer than what makes you comfortable, but it's been there before, and it'll be there again. Just believe.

Worksheet:
There's always something around the corner

 ## ONE THING TO REMEMBER

When the money starts to run out, have faith it'll come back.
But also work your ass off to make that more possible.

 ## ONE THING TO DO

Think about what you really, really, really want to do for your next project.
Write down three possibilities.

1

2

3

Who will you tell about it?

How will you let them know?

THE THIRD WUW
SHARE

Where you may be on your own but you're never alone

This UDOT thing can get exhausting. To say we wear many hats would be an understatement. The burden is huge.

When I ask other UDOTs what surprises them about being out on their own, one thing I hear over and over is how physically and emotionally tiring it can be. Part of that may be time management, and part may be wanting to succeed so badly that you'll do anything and everything, everywhere, all the time, to prove that you can do it all.

We have endless responsibilities constantly circling around the actual work. There's the enormous time and energy it takes to get the work, which could be a full time job. Then there's all of the administrative duties, hiring and keeping employees, finding office space, doing the financial and legal diligence, all of the business-y stuff that *also* takes so much time.

The kicker? We're not very experienced, instinctively adept, or even interested in that stuff.

But my fellow UDOTs, there are people out there. They're smart, talented, experienced, and waiting to help you. Friends, family, former classmates or workmates. Other UDOTs and good old non-UDOTs, sitting on Go. Give it some thought. It's amazing how many resources you'll realize you have. This is at the heart of the third **W**ay UDOTs **W**in.

As a UDOT, you may be on your own, but you're never alone.

You don't have to do it all yourself. In fact, you shouldn't. It's much better if you don't. There will always be people to share your burden. Usually because they like you, and sometimes, because you pay them. Either way, it makes things better when you realize you're not out here all alone.

Throw out a signal. Someone will send you a line.

Chapter 10:
Hug a client

If you watched the seminal TV show *Mad Men*, you know the contempt Don Draper had for his clients. It pretty much dripped from his well-pressed suits. He saw them as a necessary evil. When I worked at agencies, I knew a lot of people who felt the same way. They didn't trust clients, they didn't believe clients really understood what they did, and they didn't think clients valued what they brought to the table. They just didn't like clients.

This may not surprise you but UDOTS LOVE CLIENTS. We always have, we always will. And not just a superficial needy love because they pay us, but a genuine love and appreciation for being in our lives. It's something very real that's hard to appreciate until you're a UDOT winning and maintaining your own clients.

I built my business with work from my former agency clients who trusted me enough to give projects to my fledgling company despite my terrible business model, which had a core strategy of "See what work people give me if I take them out to lunch enough." All these years later, those clients still provide the vast majority of my business. In fact, most small business owners report that over half of their revenue comes from repeat customers.[2]

Equally crucial is putting that genuine and sincere love for clients into action. It's kind of like courting someone who you hope will date you forever. I

---

[2] http://blog.biakelsey.com/index.php/2014/04/03/biakelsey-and-manta-joint-report-smbs-shift-priority-to-customer-retention/

periodically send clients notes and articles that are relevant to their businesses. I send holiday gifts, and sometimes I'll send little presents for birthdays or promotions. On the simple Excel spreadsheet where I keep track of my top contacts, I have a space for notes where I store information relevant to the gift-giving ("loved the banana bread," "twins Samantha /Jeremy born March 2013").

And most important, I take advantage of every possible opportunity to hang with a client socially, eat a good meal, and have fun. I can't get enough of it because it almost always leads somewhere good. It could be a new project, some stories to swap, or just a nice hug. Since I really love my clients, they all sound pretty good to me. The food's just a bonus.

Worksheet:
Hug a client

 ## ONE THING TO REMEMBER

Constantly and actively find ways to show clients your love and appreciation, in ways that feel comfortable for you.

 ## ONE THING TO DO

Ask a client (and/or potential client) about his or her family, pets, travel plans, favorite restaurant/vacation spot/book/movie/music. What questions will you ask to get the ball rolling?

1

2

3

4

5

Other

Chapter 11:
Get hitched

As a fiercely independent thinker with a sometimes unnecessarily prideful (i.e. ego-heavy) spirit, creating a professional partnership has been one of the hardest things for me to do (and it's still a work in progress). I know how beneficial it would be to share the burden of getting new work, the challenge of thinking through the work, and the joy of successfully creating great work. But because of how I think and the way I approach the world, it's hard for me to let go and trust someone to be my business partner.

You may be different, one of many UDOTs who have a natural ability to form partnerships and can't operate without one. Or you may feel the need to do it all on your own, whether it's driven by pride, selfishness, control freak-ness, and/or a burning desire to prove yourself after you've been separated from a job. When I got laid off I instantly shifted into "something to prove" mode, and with that came a stubborn insistence to do it all on my own. Until I learned better.

There are endless benefits for UDOTs to find partners when we're out on our own. The work will always be better when you have another brain to push yours around. Opposing opinions, cognitive dissonance, and good old-fashioned arguments will all have a positive effect on any work you do, because it will force you to look at things differently, which could lead you to unexpected answers. Zach Friedlander, founder of the Aloha Poke restaurant chain, spoke the truth when he said, "If you're the smartest guy in the room, you're in the wrong room." Plus, you'll have more fun when you share experiences with someone else, even (maybe especially) when the experiences are kind of harrowing. If for no other reason, it'll give you someone to fart around with, or just plain fart around.

If it really doesn't feel right, you can try hitching yourself to more than one person at a time: having a revolving stable of partners, like a horse at a breeding farm (without the, y'know, breeding).

For the first three years of Twist's existence, Jennifer Johnson worked part time with me. We had worked together at my last ad agency, where she was a phenomenal account manager, keeping the balls in the air and making sure everything happened as it should. She did the same thing for Twist—and endured my many quirks—and it was just the kind of help I needed to get Twist off the ground. For the next three years I wanted to find my way into new areas of expertise, and I partnered with innovation expert Joe Kim. Joe helped me expand Twist into product and service innovation projects, something I never could have done on my own. For the next few years, instead of partnering with one person, I worked with a variety of partners, getting to share each others' brains, putting the right people on the right projects, and fortunately, doing great work.

Even when the work is great, the relationship may suck. And sometimes the output won't match the excellence of the relationship. If the partnership doesn't work you can always separate, with little acrimony (and no alimony), a ton of good stuff you learned from each other, and lots of inside jokes.

As in life, there will be tradeoffs—independence for increased capabilities, shared fees for shared responsibility, ownership for partnership. It's hard to let go of total control, to forego fatter fees, to share the glory. But it's so worth it, because the end product will be that much better. And that's what will lead you to the next great project.

Worksheet:
Get hitched

 ## ONE THING TO REMEMBER

Find a partner to share your challenges, failures, and successes, even if it's temporary or part time.

 ## ONE THING TO DO

Who can you see yourself partnering with? Write the name of…

Someone who makes perfect sense for you to partner with tomorrow:

Someone who makes no sense for you to partner with, might drive you crazy, but may also force you to think differently:

Someone who you don't know but admire from near or far, who would be cool to meet and even potentially work with were you to reach out to that person and have that person say "Sure, let's talk" because, hey, you never know.

THEN CALL THAT PERSON. NOW. NOT LATER. NOW.

Chapter 12:
Get professional help

Don't do it alone.

Some people slide into opportunities to ask for help the way baby ducks slide into water: going to meet-ups and comfortably splashing around with new friends, finding coaches to learn from and peers to coach, helping each other out and making each other better. Other people (as I look in the mirror) feel like they're not really doing the entrepreneurial thing "right" if they're not doing it alone.

That was me when I started, but not now. I've been working with an executive coach since I started Twist and I still talk to him three or four times a year. He's especially helpful when I'm hit with a tough work or personal challenge, a financial dry spell, or just need a little "attaboy" (or a swift kick in the pants). If that's too formal (or expensive) for you, lean on friends or family to serve that role. You can also seek out other UDOTs facing similar challenges and take turns providing a shoulder to cry on.

Professional groups like the Entrepreneurs Organization (EO) and Vistage are amazing at providing advice and support for small business owners. Brian Waspi, who started and runs both online and brick and mortar businesses that cater to lovers of the outdoors, said "The #1 best decision I ever made as a UDOT was joining EO. It's been crucial for me to be able to help and learn from other UDOTs, share pains and successes, and find my tribe."

Like Brian, many of the UDOTs I interviewed were members of at least one of those organizations and could not say enough about how important they were to their survival as humans and business owners. There are certain requirements to join, like revenue minimums. If you don't qualify, consider starting your own professional support group. Mastermind groups are one example, providing advice and a similar experience in a less formal (and less expensive) way. I started an eight-person Mastermind group and it's been incredibly helpful to our members for topics like business development, writing proposals, computing fees, and social media and digital expertise.

Then there's good old networking. I used to think of networking events like a tornado: I could never tell if the people running towards them were brave or just plain crazy. I didn't have confidence that networking events worked for me so I seldom went. When I did, I usually felt a crushing sense of impending futility as soon as I walked in the door and a visceral, skin-crawling, full-body need to leave within milliseconds.

I'm better now. How'd I get there?

Sometimes it's simply about having the right attitude. Being optimistic. This comes easy for some people, like Becky Galvez, whose company designs custom neckwear and Hawaiian shirts. "I love everyone I meet," Becky said. "I love connecting with people and helping people. If I could make a business of that it's what I'd do!" I love her attitude. I'm also a little jealous of it.

It's also about learning how to network better. Networking worked better for me once I figured out how to pick and choose the right events where I could meet people with attitudes I relate to and skills I value. There are often different chapters within a large organization and one in the city might fit you better than one in the suburbs, or one that meets at lunch may be better than one that meets early in the morning. Meetup.com has hundreds of meetups where you can find like-minded people with similar interests. If you see an event that interests you, look at the invite list to see if they feel like your people. Do a little internet snooping before you commit to an event. As soon as I was able to figure out which groups to join and which events to go to, they became incredibly productive. And surprisingly enjoyable.

Don't be proud, be smart. Get help, whether it's professional or more casual. Go eat with old friends, buy lunch for new friends, talk to a coach, see a shrink. Brainstorm and build something together. Communicate and collaborate; I guarantee each of you will raise your game.

Worksheet:
Get professional help

 ## ONE THING TO REMEMBER

If you're ever stuck, you'll never regret asking for help.

 ## ONE THING TO DO

What three potential resources that could help strengthen you and your business would you be comfortable tapping into tomorrow?

1

2

3

What three potential resources that could strengthen you and your business but might also make your skin crawl, heart pound and palms sweat just thinking about, would you be comfortable trying…sometime…soon…?

1

2

3

OK, Nice job. Now, the next step. Send a text or email, make a call. Get in touch. Don't delay.

Chapter 13:
Be unapologetically loyal

Sameness is boring for a lot of people, and especially for UDOTs. We're voracious challenge-chasers in search of the next great problem that'll set our hair on fire and drive us to solve it in our distinctively brilliant way. That aversion to sameness can also lead us to constantly seek new resources, in the interest of new approaches and new solutions.

For UDOT success, consider going the other way. Whether it's the developer who brings your ideas to life in a mobile app or the guy who cuts your hair, a clerk or project manager or accountant, try to hire the same people over and over. Find long term partners you trust implicitly, who will bail you out when you have little to no money or time to get a project done (or a big unexpected meeting and a bad hair day). Think of those Friday 4:00 PM client calls, asking for something by Monday morning. When that happens, who you gonna call?

When I was an ad agency creative director, while a lot of my peers liked working with the hottest new editor, I tried to work as often as possible with a great editor named James Lipetzky. We did excellent work together for a 15-year period, after which he moved to Los Angeles and I started Twist. Five years later he sent me an email asking if I wanted to find a way to partner again. It led to the creation of our video content subsidiary called Visualize, providing a service to our existing clients that we didn't have before. And the best part was, the work came easily and we did it well because of our history together.

I'm not saying you should always work with the same people exclusively. It's good to have a variety of resources for a greater breadth of creativity and fresh thinking. Make a list, broken down by categories of potential partners, from which you can choose liberally and joyfully. But also make sure there's someone in every category you can return to repeatedly.

My favorite-ever boss had a long-running relationship with the maitre d' at a classic Chicago restaurant and advertising hangout, and he had a table permanently waiting for him where he would woo clients. Years later, taking a cue from him, I became friends with the host at a great lunch spot that clients loved and was impossible to reserve. Those relationships allowed two pretty unfancy guys to impress people when impressing needed to be done.

Whether it's connecting over great food or collaborating on great work, having a history and a common language with a longtime partner is invaluable. When you speak the same language you can move more quickly and push each other to unexplored areas without ill will, and have inside jokes that just make it more goshdarn fun. Embrace sameness, not all the time, but often. Loyalty is a great gap-bridger, one of the best creativity-inducing and most powerful business-building tools in the world.

Worksheet:
Be unapologetically loyal

 # ONE THING TO REMEMBER

Keep your friends close and your trusted partners closer.

 # ONE THING TO DO

Think of ten smart, funny, creative, helpful-in-their-own-way people that you know and either have worked with or would like to work with, who could provide some kind of benefit to your business, as weird and tangential as it might be. Write why they'd be good partners.

1

2

3

4

5

6

7

8

9

10

Now go ahead and invite them to lunch.

STOP COUNTING MONEY,
START COUNTING FRIENDS.

Chapter 14:
Stop counting money and start counting friends

When you worry more about money, you just might get more money…but you also might get more ulcers, cold sores, acid reflux, and shortness of breath. You'll get less sleep too, so you'll have that going for you.

Instead, focus on relationships, making connections, and building a network. When you have a list of go-to potential clients, the work will follow and the money will come. It doesn't need to be a huge list; sometimes all it takes is a core group of trusted partners big enough to sustain you when one of them goes away. Even then, they'll still be around to give you referrals, which is as good as their repeat business.

Your network is the key to getting work and building a business over time vs. just getting a project here and there. Put that list in a place where you'll see it every day and check it twice. Or more, if it helps. Money comes from people, not companies. Collect your people and stay up to date on them.

But remember this ridiculously important fact about a network: it's not just about making and building it, it's about maintaining and extending it. Your network is a living, breathing, and hopefully constantly growing organism that injects oxygen into every UDOT's life. Networking isn't a "Phew, I can check that box!" thing, because staying on someone's radar means being top of mind when a project comes up. It's the box that keeps getting unchecked once you check it. Being connected is an always thing, not a one-time thing.

How will you know when you haven't been networking enough? When the phone stops ringing.

Worksheet:
Stop counting money and start counting friends

 ONE THING TO REMEMBER

Look at your contact list at least every other day and call or send a note to someone you haven't connected with in over six months.

 ONE THING TO DO

To get you started, get in touch with two people every day for the next five business days. Who will they be?

Monday   Thursday
1   1
2   2

Tuesday   Friday
1   1
2   2

Wednesday
1
2

GET SOMEONE
ELSE TO DO THE
STUFF YOU

Chapter 15:
Get someone else to do the stuff you suck at

When I surveyed clients about the first thing they do when they receive a proposal, the majority said they go to the last page to see what will be delivered and how much it'll cost. Then they go back and read through the whole proposal with a fine-toothed brain, lingering on every bullet point to make sure they understand how they'll be spending their money. If laying out those details isn't something you do well, DON'T DO IT YOURSELF. Hire someone who does.

As a UDOT you're probably great at one thing and can do a couple of other things pretty well. For everything else, you should hire someone else.

Tim Frick, who owns the digital marketing agency Mightybytes, attributes his success to "learning what I'm not good at and finding people who do it well and putting them into place. If you try to do everything you'll go crazy. You'll resent your business."

Since the day I started Twist, I've trusted a brilliant person named Susie Rashid to help me make more money on every project. Susie was the CFO of my last agency. She actually laid me off! But I'll never forget the kind and generous way that she did it. Once she left that agency for her own UDOT adventure, she continued to be brilliant and is even more compassionate. Her number was the first one I called the day I had to send my first proposal to a potential client.

Starting that day, for an extremely fair fee, she's been my advisor on all things financial. Just about every time I write a proposal, I leave the line blank where the fee goes, and send it to Susie. She reads through the proposal and tells me what she thinks I should charge. It's usually somewhere between 25-50% more than what I would have charged myself. Thanks to her, I charge higher fees than I ever would've considered. Hallelujah! Thank you Susie! You helped me buy new underwear and socks way sooner than I otherwise would have.

Focus on the things you're good at. For everything else, hire somebody. Eventually you'll get better at the things you suck at, maybe even good enough to do some of them yourself. But until then, find a Susie, or a Bob or a Vijay— someone who does them well—to do them for you. It'll be worth every penny.

Worksheet:
Get someone else to do the stuff you suck at

 ONE THING TO REMEMBER

Pay someone to do the business-related things you're not good at it. It'll be the best money you ever spend.

 ONE THING TO DO

Get the names of at least two UDOTs who are really good at something you're not good at (e.g., lawyers, accountants, insurance agents, web designers, writers). Call them and let them know that someday you'll ask for help with some of your business-oriented tasks. How do you find this person? Ask around. People are happy to help.

THE FOURTH WUW

DO IT!

Where you hunker down and get things done

One way to guarantee not succeeding is to not do anything, which a lot of people are pretty good at. If you actually do something, your chances of success greatly improve. That should be a scientific theory somewhere.

All kinds of hurdles stop us in our tracks. Fear of failure, the chase for perfection, or a lack of any number of things, including funds, partners, organization, vision, and good old confidence. All this can lead to paralyzing inaction.

Then there's the part where none of that matters. Where the only thing that does is taking action. Where we tell each other to step up, stand up, walk out, hit send, push play, open your eyes, hold your breath and take the leap. This is the fourth **W**ay **UDOT**s **W**in.

It's comprised of specific actions you can use to start living as a UDOT. Some you might be doing already, some might surprise you. What's most important is doing something. Even when it's so daunting it makes your head and/or stomach hurt.

Men and women dreamed about space travel for centuries until they finally had the tools and technology at their disposal. Then they figured out how to do it, and a man walked on the moon.

The tools you need are at your disposal. Get going and start doing.

DON'T PREPARE FOR MEETINGS | 🎤

SEARCH NOW   FEELIN' LUCKY

Chapter 16:
Don't prepare for meetings

Of all of the ridiculous things I have or haven't done in the years I've somehow succeeded in business, the ridiculous-est may be the way I (don't) prepare for meetings with new prospects. Does that make sense or does it make your brain hurt?

Some UDOTs diligently prepare for meetings in advance, doing extensive internet searches on potential clients, digging up common connections on LinkedIn, finding out their favorite foods and zodiac signs. There's a simpler, more productive way. It's called Active Listening.

The only "prep" I do takes place five minutes beforehand in my car or down the hall from my meeting. Praise the iPhone, all glory to Wi-Fi! It usually consists of feverish online surfing about the person I'm meeting and her company and background before I head in full of optimism despite a lack of information.

When you don't over-prepare, you don't over-postulate. You go in without bias, and it enables you to do the most important thing you can do in that type of meeting: actively listen. Lean in, put your cochlea to work, get physically closer, commit full-on to the speaker, ask great questions that show you're fully engaged. It doesn't mean you shouldn't prepare yourself with basic information. You should be able to answer questions about their business and category, and have an opinion. But it's equally important to learn what ails and excites them. Let them do the talking. You do the asking and listening so you can then start solving. You're there to help them, not the other way around.

When you actively listen, it's amazing how quickly you can pick up on the key factors in someone's challenges, which helps you start speaking the same language and develop a connection. Take the five minutes beforehand—or 10, or 15 if you need—to gain the basic knowledge you need to not look like a dummy, then go in with ears wide open. Blow them away with your ability to hear and understand their pain, and start helping to ease it with your brilliance.

Worksheet:
Don't prepare for meetings

 ## ONE THING TO REMEMBER

When it comes to new business meetings, you don't have to have all the right answers as long as you can actively listen and ask a lot of good questions.

 ## ONE THING TO DO

Practice active listening. In at least one conversation every day, whether with friends, family or co-workers, be intentional about leaning in and paying extra attention. Ask more questions than you usually would. Record the information in your brain, then on the page below, and use it in your next conversation with that person.

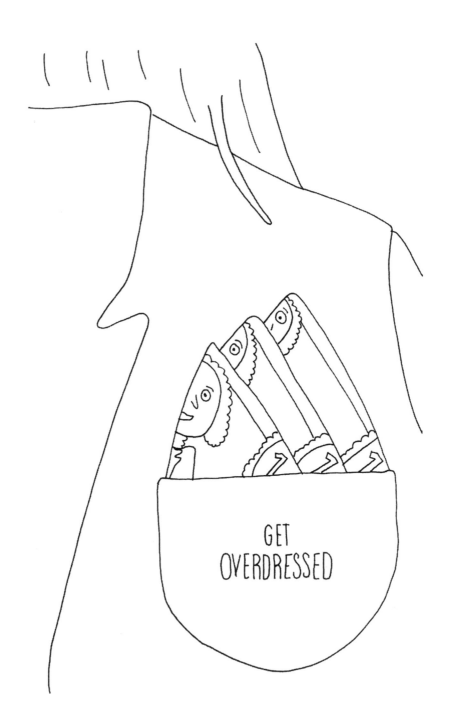

Chapter 17:
Get overdressed

This one's simple: When in doubt, wear the sport coat, skirt, or suit. Better to be dressy than messy.

As comfortable as we might be in yoga pants, shorts, t-shirts and flip-flops, and as much as our out-of-the-mainstream office existence entitles us to a life without slacks, suits, sport coats, and dresses, when I show up underdressed to a meeting I feel like a child hoping for someone's approval. When I show up overdressed I feel like a grown-up who can speak with authority and validate the more-money-I'd-like-to-charge because I have my big-boy pants on.

It's not always the case, and it may not be true in every industry, but for the most part, if we're going to feel uncomfortable, we might as well make more money doing it.

Just saying.

Worksheet:
Get overdressed

 # ONE THING TO REMEMBER

When in doubt, it's better from a business perspective to be over vs. under dressed.

 # ONE THING TO DO

Find a store and/or website that has clothes you look great in, get on their mailing list, wait until they have a sale, then splurge on something that makes you look great.

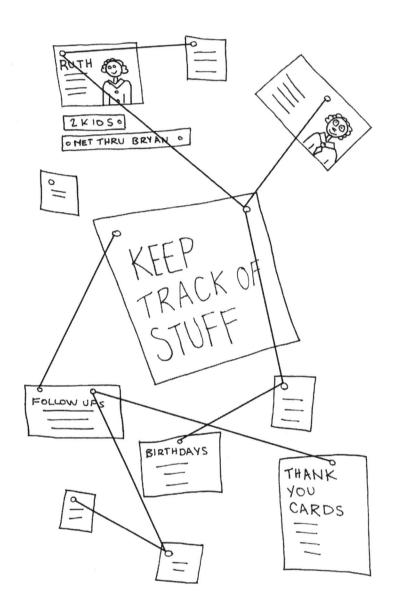

Chapter 18:
Keep track of stuff

When it comes to finding our way to new prospects and projects, I'm a huge believer in fate. You'll experience "Hey I just got a new client without really trying!" moments just by spending time at your local coffee shop or on the bleachers of your kid's soccer game and shooting the breeze with liked-minded people. That said, if we allow fate to work as a solo act, we're shortchanging our potential.

It's easy to walk away from a meeting with a new business prospect and say to ourselves, "That was awesome! I wonder when he'll call with my next billion-dollar project? Shortly, I'm sure!" Except for the part where that's not going to happen. It's on us. So after a meeting with a new prospect, do something to remind yourself that the meeting actually happened to make sure you follow-up appropriately. I have a ridiculously simple spreadsheet that keeps track of who I met with, when we met, where that person works, and when I should follow up, as well as some space for notes. If you don't do it, it's kind of like the meeting never existed, and you've wasted your time and, more important, theirs.

Judy Teibloom-Mishkin, a Maternal Child Nurse and board-certified Lactation Consultant, talked about the importance of keeping track of stuff. "You have to have self-discipline," she said. "If you're not the kind of person who can create your own structure, then this UDOT life might not for you. When you balance it with your creativity, all will be good!"

The options seem to grow daily and are as close as your phone, with lots of handy apps and software like Trello, Insightly, Wrike, Salesforce, and

Calendly. Each does slightly different things and they have varying levels of complexity. What's most important is finding the one that works for you.

For me, it's best to do my record keeping immediately after I have a meeting or phone call to make sure I remember everything important. You can also try to block out regular time each day or week to do the diligence necessary to make sure you don't run into someone in line at the coffee shop and say, "Hey, we should get together," and he says, "We did, two years, seven months, and four days ago, and you said you'd follow up with me, but who's counting?"

Relying on fate is awesome when it works out, but percentage-wise, fate has a pretty dismal track record. So give fate a hand. Keep track of stuff.

Worksheet:
Keep track of stuff

 # ONE THING TO REMEMBER

If you don't keep track of your conversations, meetings, and business development, you might as well not do any of them.

 # ONE THING TO DO

Create a record keeping method (with the amount of diligence that fits your style) to keep track of your new business efforts, and remember to update it every week.

Kinda like the one below. What will yours look like?

NAME	COMPANY	MOST RECENT	NEXT DATE	NOTES
MARY GORD	GORD & CO	2/5/18	5/5/18	HAS EXISTING CAMPAIGN WANTS TO REFRESH
REGINA VAN GELD	RBL	12/3/17		LOVES STAN'S DONUTS
FRANK REEF	CORNA COFFEE	4/5/18	6/3/18	REFERRED BY MARY GORD
ARTY GOODAN	JERBOAN	3/23/18	4/7/18	MAY EXPAND TO SECOND LINE OF PRODUCTS
JUAN ELIO	PARDO	2/16/18	2/25/18	SOCIAL CAMPAIGN
DEANNE BLACK	GLASSIC WINE	1/4/18		REFERRED BY TORY KING

REPEAT WHAT WORKS
REPEAT WHAT WORKS
REPEAT WHAT WORKS
REPEAT WHAT WORKS
REPEAT WHAT WORKS
REPEAT WHAT WORKS
REPEAT WHAT WORKS
REPEAT WHAT WORKS
REPEAT WHAT WORKS
REPEAT WHAT WORKS
REPEAT WHAT WORKS
REPEAT WHAT WORKS
REPEAT WHAT WORKS
REPEAT WHAT WORKS
REPEAT WHAT WORKS
REPEAT WHAT WORKS
REPEAT WHAT WORKS
REPEAT WHAT WORKS
REPEAT WHAT WORKS

Chapter 19:
Repeat what works

"I don't know how I get the jobs I get. Sometimes it happens, sometimes it doesn't. It's usually just a matter of sending a proposal and crossing my fingers." I can't tell you how many times UDOTs have talked about getting projects in those terms.

I understand.

In the early days of Twist's existence, every time a client said "Yes!" to a new project, I felt giddiness that it was actually happening—and then dreaded uncertainty that it would never happen again. I didn't know what to do to erase that feeling of not knowing. The best answer I had was "send proposal, cross fingers" with no thought to how I might improve my hit rate. It's not a very good answer (and it's a terrible business model!). The simple truth is, if you do nothing to keep the phone ringing other than cross your fingers, get used to nothing, because it's what you'll start experiencing more and more.

While I don't have anything that remotely looks like a complex sales system, I do make a point of repeating the things that I know have helped me nail down projects. Early on, it was tiering my projects into phases, so clients could see how long it would take and how much it would cost to do part A, part B, and so on. It helped them understand the specific work they were getting for what they were spending. As I learned more about how to apply my value to a client's needs, especially in a marketing world that can often produce hard to measure results, I was able to address ROI (Return on Investment) in a way that allowed clients to justify hiring me, which helped loosen their sphincters a bit. I always do both of those things now. Both are great ways to help get clients to sign on the dotted line.

Take stock and write down lessons learned, what did and didn't work after a meeting, case, experiment, or project. Mike Stratta is a longtime UDOT who owns a digital marketing agency. For him, one specific step does the trick: "I've found a way that works for my brain and if I deviate from it I find myself three to four days off the trail and it's hard to make my way back. It's crucial to not just make a list, but get it off the page and onto the calendar right away." For Mike, writing on a piece of paper is fine. Doing it with expediency is what makes it work.

UDOTs are constantly tinkering and experimenting. If you can capture the steps you take when you're successful, you'll decrease time spent and increase jobs won. Use a Post-It or your favorite on-line tool; keep a running list of "dos" and "don'ts." Put these invaluable business-sustaining pearls of wisdom on the wall or tattoo them onto your arm.

Whatever you do, keep your systems somewhere you'll be forced to look at them regularly. They're easy to forget about in the rush to move on to the next project, which is exactly when you need to remember them. If you're able to repeat those things again and again, it'll help the giddiness outweigh the dreadedness.

Worksheet:
Repeat what works

 # ONE THING TO REMEMBER

When it comes to getting (and keeping) new business, figure out what works for you and keep doing it.

 # ONE THING TO DO

These things have really helped you get, keep, and grow business in the past so you should probably keep doing them:

1

2

3

4

5

Can you do one of them now? I bet you can.

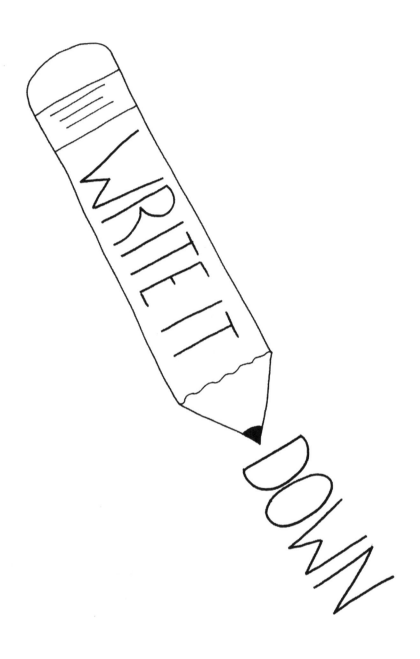

Chapter 20:
Write it down (NOW!)

If you're stewing on a challenge while you're out on a run or in the shower or driving in your car, I guarantee two things: At some point something great will pop into your head, and if you don't immediately capture it, you'll lose it.

Actually, you may remember it. But instead of emanating the sheer brilliant luminescence it had when you first thought of it, it will have something to do with llamas. This is especially true when you're sleeping; genius will come to you and it will be beautiful and I promise you, regardless of how crystal clear it was in the middle of the night, IT WILL NOT BE THE SAME IN THE MORNING.

So whether it's in the middle of the night or the middle of a meeting, decide how you'll be sure to capture your brilliant ideas. I use a combination of the Apple Notes app, the QuickVoice Pro app (push record and talk, great for when you can't use your hands, like driving and dog-walking), and a good old fashioned pad and pencil I keep on the dresser near my bed. When inspiration strikes me in the middle of the night, I grab that pad and write standing up so I don't fall asleep while I'm writing, and move the pencil down the page as I write so I don't write over words. Once in a while it looks like hieroglyphics, but the vast majority of the time, it's legible enough.

There may be times when you capture your thoughts as they come out of your brain, and when you look at them the next day they read like hieroglyphics. They make no sense or simply aren't very good. That's ok. They still may be something you can build on if you stare at them long enough. If you don't get into the practice of writing everything down, you will lose great stuff. And you can be entertained by the stuff that reads like hieroglyphics.

Whatever app, software or device you need to capture your thoughts, keep it by your bed, in your car, in your purse, or in your pocket, to help make sure your brilliant thoughts don't fade into the ether and you don't wake up and say "Llamas…?"

Worksheet:
Write it down (NOW!)

 ONE THING TO REMEMBER

Write down any brilliant thought you have even if you're sure you'll remember it, because if you don't, you won't.

 ONE THING TO DO

Your go-to ways of capturing ideas :

1

2

3

Chapter 21:
Never underestimate the power of free food

When I was little, my Dad, who owned a small electrical contracting business in Chicago, sent three-foot long kosher salamis and tins of pistachios to his clients every Christmas. It was a memorable, high-quality treat and all they talked about until the following Christmas (other than all the business they were doing together).

I wore out my credit card in the early days of Twist, paying for anyone who'd meet me for coffee, lunch, dinner or drinks. Those encounters proved triply fruitful: we had great food and drinks, we had great conversation, and many of those kale and caffeine-fueled meetings eventually led to great work. Sometimes that person had a project we could work on right away, sometimes it wouldn't turn into actual work until 18 months later, sometimes it didn't lead directly to any work but to a great new connection that then led to work. It's hard to always draw a straight line from a food-fueled interaction to a paid engagement. But food-related gestures, even small ones like sending a little treat at major holidays or even minor ones (hello Groundhog Day), can do wonders for UDOTs, and I do it a lot. Amazon Prime loves me.

If you can't get a client to engage with you face to face over food, go to a food-focused site like Zingermans.com, or your own favorite online food emporium, and start slinging vittles through the ether until their bellies are full and their business is yours. This not a shameless plug for Zingerman's, the single best most amazing food emporium in the world, it's a plea to remember the wonderful persuasiveness of free food.

If investing in relationships is the single best networking and business building tool, then investing in salamis and nuts isn't too far behind.

Worksheet:
Never underestimate the power of free food

 # ONE THING TO REMEMBER

Food is the most acceptable form of bribery in the world.

 # ONE THING TO DO

Again, this is not a shameless plug for Zingerman's (zingermans.com), but man they know how to make (and package and ship) unique, amazing, impossible-not-to-please-potential-clients food, so you could do a lot worse than sending their stuff to someone you want to impress.*

At a minimum, the next time you have a meeting that involves food or drink, pick up the check!

*PS, dear Zingerman's: Please send all discounts and free food to danny@twistyourthinking.com

THE FIFTH WUW
ENJOY IT

Where you get to do more of what you love and less of what you hate

We're UDOTs by choice.

We do it because we want to, not because we have to.

Well, actually, we have to find a way to make money so we can pay bills and eat food. But we could get a job working for someone else.

We do this UDOT thing because we want the control, freedom, and flexibility that go with it. And since it comes with a huge burden of responsibility, it should also come with a huge amount of enjoyment.

If we're going to put out the effort to brave the uncertainty of being out on our own, and work through all the challenges unique to being a UDOT, shouldn't we squeeze every nanosecond of happiness out of it when we can?

This **W**ay UDOTs **W**in is the shortest chapter, has the fewest actual tips for UDOT success, and is maybe the most important WUW of all. It provides reminders of the importance of enjoying ourselves, having fun, and treating ourselves to the goodies that we've earned. We only get to do this life thing once—as far as we know—and for us UDOTs, there may be nothing more important than enjoying the life we've created for ourselves. Justifying all the hard work by doing the things we love to do. Consciously, purposefully, and lovingly.

Why bother trying to survive all of the inherent dangers of traveling through the universe if you don't get to bounce up and down on the moon?

WITH
YOURSELF

Chapter 22:
Play with yourself

As a UDOT, it's not just good to play with yourself, it's imperative.

Maybe your mother told you you'll go blind if you do it, but I say you'll be able to see things better. Time to be alone with ourselves and explore is a precious luxury unique to UDOTs. People who work in structured corporate cultures don't often get to experience those wonderful and valuable stretches of insanely productive time.

Take advantage of that time and space to play. Allow yourself to get distracted. Step away from your work. Walk the dog, shoot baskets, play music or solitaire or chess, watch your favorite reality TV show, sing karaoke. Play a game on your favorite addictive mindless app, listen to Anna Faris's unique *Unqualified* podcast, read Seth Godin's blog. Go to a movie or concert or baseball game in the middle of the day.

I love to plan vacations that may or may not actually happen. My brain gets energy from visiting americanairlines.com, my pulse quickens when I go to sites for hotels and restaurants I want to visit, mountains I want to hike, places where I can do yoga on the beach.

Kate Kimmerle is a UDOT who runs a cosmetics company and actually does get away. For her, inspiration comes from "getting on a plane and going somewhere. My best moments of true clarity come when I get away from the business. I need to be somewhere with a blank notepad, where I can zone out."

Remember how important it is to smile and laugh. Power down your brain and pump up your heart. Do anything that entertains you. Enjoy what makes you happy because it'll reflect back on the work you do and make you better at it.

If you want additional first-hand proof, check out the volumes of positivity literature available to the world. One great repository for a lot of that information, and an easy read with great actionable tips, is Gretchen Rubin's *The Happiness Project*. And if you prefer your encouragement in video form, check out the crazy funny and inspiring TedTalk from Shawn Achor on the Happy Secret to Better Work.[3]

In the midst of all of the stresses of work, remember to let yourself get excited about something. You work your butt off so let your brain benefit from it. Carve out time to indulge your playful side. It helps those stresses float away and leads to "Where'd that come from?!?" thinking. And boy does that feel good.

---

[3] https://www.ted.com/talks/shawn_achor_the_happy_secret_to_better_work

Worksheet:
Play with yourself

 ONE THING TO REMEMBER

Not everyone has the flexibility to block out chunks of alone time every once in a while, but UDOTs do. Make good use of these golden opportunities.

 ONE THING TO DO

Schedule some time to play with yourself. Put it on your calendar. Like this:

S	M	T	W	T	F	S
		MOVIE W/CHRIS	FLIGHT CONCERT			HIKE W/ANNE
				CUBS GAME		
	YOGA				GAME NIGHT	BREW TRIP

Chapter 23:
Stretch 'til it hurts

Pushing ourselves into uncomfortable places is one of the most important things a UDOT can do. Discomfort is a painful necessity; it means we're growing. A lot of us go out on our own so we can do things our way, but that doesn't mean we can sit back and do nothing but count money. It actually puts an increased need for diligence on our shoulders to continually improve. It's easy to sit back and rest on what you know; it's also a good way to become stagnant and roadkillian.

Discomfort is in this chapter about enjoying what we do because nothing feels better than getting better at something, and pushing ourselves out of our comfort zone is a great way to get better at something. Upping our game, gaining new skills. It's one of the happiest things a UDOT can do. It provides the magical double whammy of helping us feel better about ourselves and opening us up to new opportunities.

Surf relentlessly, network fearlessly, and read endlessly. Reach out to new people and groups and learn something whenever possible. Go to classes and events and conferences, push yourself to talk to people even when you'd rather get root canal. Gain new skills, new knowledge, and new friends, because new information and new connections are the lifeblood of our existence. It's like working any muscle; it can be uncomfortable, it can be hard work, it takes time and patience, but it'll be worth it, because it'll make you exponentially stronger.

One thing this meant for me has been raising my "tech" game over the years. When I came out of the corporate world the highlight of my computer skills was to create a Word document, so there's been a good deal of pain involved as I've stretched my abilities. I spent so much time in the first few months of Twist's existence in the Apple Store learning new skills, I knew every person who worked there, and boy did they know me. I pushed myself and learned how to create proposals and spread sheets, and I even designed my own website. It was pretty bad, but it felt pretty great.

For some UDOTs, our big stretch has been learning to be our own accountant: trying our hand at payroll, investigating online accounting systems, and establishing ourselves as an LLC. For web designer Keith Glantz, whose design shop won't stop growing, it's about keeping up: "I worry about becoming a dinosaur. Not learning. So I'm always reading about trends in my business. When do I do it? 5–6 AM, 11–12 PM. Whenever I can."

For most UDOTs I've met, the idea of continuing education and keeping up with information as the world speeds forward—and even getting ahead of it— is as crucial as it is painful, be it through formal programs or books borrowed from the library.

One more important thing: get your body stretching physically too. Run, walk, bike, spin, swim, practice Qi Gong, play extreme table tennis, whatever works for you. Just make sure you work on it. The body and the mind are eternally connected.

Worksheet:
Stretch 'til it hurts

 ## ONE THING TO REMEMBER

Forcing yourself to stretch can be intimidating to your psyche and painful for your body, but when you're done you feel good, you look good, and when it comes to work, man, can you ever do good.

 ## ONE THING TO DO

Three ways I could stretch my brain and/or body that I've done a good job avoiding but ok already, I'll do it:

1

2

3

The one I'll commit to doing within the next 24 hours:

1

Chapter 24:
Embrace FONBO

If one word defines the cultural zeitgeist of the early 21st century, it might be FOMO, an acronym that stands for Fear of Missing Out, defined by Merriam-Webster as "Fear of not being included in something (such as an interesting or enjoyable activity) that others are experiencing."

To remind myself of why I became a UDOT, I created a more appropriate acronym: FONBO. It stands for Fear of Not Being Original. It's pretty much the reason why we head down the UDOT path: The desire to create our own thing, our way, with passion and pride and joy.

Dan Hogan founded and runs Medalogix, a company focused on better outcomes in home health care and hospice. He and his company do great work. Embracing FONBO may have something to do with it. "There's a freedom of creativity to being your own boss," Dan said. "I can creatively explore new aspects of the business. Think about new ideas. It's wholly invigorating to have that autonomy. If I want to explore building this cool thing, look into the future, I have the ability to do that."

Just remember one important fact: Originality is awesome, but so is paying the bills, and as a business owner, you'll most likely be working for other people. There's no reason why you can't be original, make money, and still express yourself in a way that feels fulfilling. It just may take a bit of compromise.

You'll get opportunities to reinvent the wheel: to create something fresh, unique, beautiful, and all yours. But there will be times—almost too many too count—when you'll have to make a wheel that a client has in mind. You may not like that wheel very much. And then you may have to modify it in ways you like even less. You may prefer it shorter or longer or bigger or smaller, different in how it's structured or organized, bought or sold, tastes, looks, or acts. You can have a spirited and respectful discussion, but ultimately, clients get what clients want. When it comes to client work, originality sometimes needs to be tempered.

Here's the big BUT: As a UDOT, you'll also have opportunities to do the things you love and care about. When you do, the work you create will be beautiful and awesome and crackle with electric originality. The more I cook and do yoga, the more I think and write.

Being able to create things that are all yours provides life-giving oxygen for anyone who's out on their own. It's up to you to create the time and space to make those opportunities come true. When you do, embrace them, bring your ideas to life in a way that makes your toes tingle, do your thing and do it well. Explore new aspects of yourself and your business. Revel in FONBO, and in your ability to express your originality. Enjoy every glorious minute.

Worksheet:
Embrace FONBO

 ONE THING TO REMEMBER

When opportunities come to do the original work that gets you most excited, let 'er rip, and rip hard.

 ONE THING TO DO

Decide on a side project that makes you really fulfilled, then jump in with both hands, feet and sides of your brain. Create time (block it out on your calendar) and space (physical or emotional) to make sure you get it done. Write down three possibilities, and circle the one you think you can start within the next two days:

1

2

3

THE SIXTH (SECRET) WUW
YOUR CHAPTER

Some restaurants have secret menus, from which only the people who know about them can order and partake and enjoy. The real secret is, they're not that secret. They're just a great way for people to feel like they're part of a tribe and have some cool inside information.

You now have your own version of a secret menu. A bunch of new WUWs in your head and tools in your hands. Go rock the world. I know you will.

In true UDOT fashion, there's something I want to ask of you.

The tools in this book are just a start. There are so many more of them out there in the world and in your brains. Time to share, UDOTs.

One of the great joys I've experienced as I've written The Worst Business Model in the World has been facilitating workshops with UDOTs based on the contents of the book. In these collaborative sessions, I start the discussion by taking the participants through the WUWs and explaining a few of the tips, and then they take it from there, offering their own, digging deeper, debating, laughing and sometimes crying. The passion UDOTs have for our craft, our businesses and each other is undeniable, and the information we have to share with each other after years of experience is invaluable. Even if you haven't been a UDOT for very long, we all have something to share. Now it's your turn.

What tips do you have for the readers of this book? They could be things you already do religiously, or things you've always wanted to try. Write them below to remind yourself, then share those great ideas. Post them everywhere online, especially on Twitter @dannyschuman and add your own hashtags. Here are a few to get you started: #UDOTS, #heyudots, #UDOTSRULE, #UDOTNATION, #worstbusinessmodel, #lifefullnobull. I can't wait to see what you come up with, and I'll share everything I get everywhere I go!

Thank you. UDOTS Rule.

One last thing

If the WUWs and tools in this book spoke to you, helped you think differently, and improved your life as a UDOT, would you take a few minutes to write a review on Amazon? Here are some starter thoughts:

"This book changed my life and the lives of everyone within a 5-mile radius of the coffee shop where I read it."

Or, "My IQ, income, and general popularity exploded immediately after reading this book."

Or something more truthful and equally complimentary.

Many positive Amazon reviews can be the lifeblood of a successful book and the backbone of a successful movement. I greatly appreciate your help!

And if you want to get freebie bonus thingys (good stuff, I promise), please sign up at heyudots.com.

Thanks so much.

Acknowledgements

Writing acknowledgements feels like penning an Oscar acceptance speech, and even with time to write these, it's possible that I'll leave someone out. If this is true of you, I promise to buy you a Zingerman's coffee cake or take you for coffee, your choice. Please let me know at danny@twistyourthinking.com.

Never ending thank-yous to:

Dawn and HL, who were excellent teachers and surprisingly good entrepreneurs.

Sarah and Joey for enduring my texts and emails, both informative and embarrassing.

Amy, Jenny, Mike and Larry for endless sibling love and encouragement.

Nola for the walks, where most of this book was recorded into my QuickVoice Pro app.

Every single one of my awesome clients.

The 100+ (and counting) UDOT interviewees.

The excellent baristas at Buzz, La Colombe, Dollop, Sip, Filter, Star Lounge, City Grounds, Coffee Studio, and the Rock House.

My Second Shift community, UDOT Mastermind group, and Soho House Breakfast Club.

People who don't know they inspired me: Danny Meyer, Jason Fried, Seth Godin, Sara Blakely, Patrick Lencioni, David Allen.

People who do: Chuck Maniscalco, Stephen Carr, Susie Rashid, Amy Krouse Rosenthal, Ellen Kellogg, Jill Salzman.

Karma, for doing your thing.

About the Author

Danny Schuman became an entrepreneur when he decided he wanted to spend more time creating things and less time in meetings. Despite knowing pretty much nothing about business, he started a marketing consultancy called Twist in 2009, in the middle of a tanking economy. Somehow, within three years, Twist earned over a million dollars in revenue and almost 10 years later, it isn't just still in business, it's thriving. Thus was born *The Worst Business Model in the World*.

As Danny grew Twist and further developed The Worst Business Model concept, he plugged into local and national entrepreneurial communities to connect with other founders and study their business opportunities and challenges. He interviewed more than 100 entrepreneurs and began speaking, teaching, and workshopping at tech incubators like 1871 and the Hatchery, at colleges and universities, as well as at many co-working spaces and entrepreneurial associations.

While he's never had any intention of making more money than he could count, he's had every intention of coaching and teaching entrepreneurs who crave the ability to turn their passions into a career. *The Worst Business Model in the World: A New Kind of Guide for a New Kind of Entrepreneur* serves as a roadmap to help entrepreneurs stay stubbornly and blissfully independent so they can spend more time doing what they love and less time doing what they hate.

Danny is a rabid baseball and Cubs fan who's been to 35 (past and present) major league ballparks. He loves being an empty nester, but don't tell his kids that. Michael Jordan called him Peanut Butter Jelly Boy, but that's a story for another time.

Made in the USA
Monee, IL
01 January 2020